Power Love
Power Life

7 Keys to A Meaningful & Fulfilling Life

Annie Lim, PhD

First Printing: 2016

ISBN 978-0-9951964-0-7

WEWorld Publishing
4-5694 Highway 7 E, Suite 366
Markham, ON, L3P 1B4

www.weworldpublishing.com

DEDICATION

To my parents, Lim Hong Chai and Kong Ong Yin,
my children, Josiah, Jordan and Joy
and my grandparents who are watching over me

CONTENTS

ACKNOWLEDGMENTS

I would like to thank my parents, Lim Hong Chai and Kong Ong Yin for their unwavering love and support for me, my children, Josiah, Jordan and Joy – my strength and joy, Zach – for his love, support and wittiness, Shirley, Brandon and my in laws, Ho Joo Mian and Tiew Siew Lian for supporting me with the kids which allows me to do what I love.

My mentors – Kerry Zurier, Dame Wendy Tan, Dwain Jeworski, Serge Gravelle, Susan Davis, Lana Holmes, Charmaine Semon, Hazel Henderson, Jyoti Prevatt, KH Lim, Allan Chen, Steven & Vivian Tay for your constant love and guidance, my coach and friend – Annie Fitzgerald for being there for me, Natalie Foong, my cousin who unknowingly started my journey of transformation, Robert McDowell, Ginelle Foskin and Joey Chung for editing and improving my book, amazing friends – Cathy Levell, Shirllin Ching, Vena Osman, Han Dang and Bernard Chen for giving me their valuable feedback about the book.

My team at WEWorld Network (Ruth Bayang, Ginelle Foskin, Serge Gravelle, Hana Bakir, Kevin Yeoh, Jana Moreno, Ruth Francis, Shirllin Ching, Han Dang, Joey Chung, Vena Osman) and WEWorld Leadership Circles globally for your trust, love and support, Miracle5 team (Jacy, Saba, Vena, Fern, Mariza, Andrew, Mira), Terence Tan, Adelene Bek, Reza Ali, Sylvia Esau, Esther Ho, Tia Nguyen, John Stamoulos, Dominique Lyone, Seattle coaching family (Deborah, Bea, Judy, Lori, Garren, Elizabeth), family members - Ricky, Si Wei, Mary, Mae, Walter, Ho De, Prudence, Lily, Andrew, Aily, Preben, Kay, Gary, Ong Hong, Kim Piew, Soo Cheng, Kim Wah, Monica, Mike, Bee Guat, Albert, Sue, Gin, Ophelia, aunties, uncles, cousins, nieces, nephews and friends including those not mentioned here whom I love and adore.

The Universe for always guiding me and supporting me to continue to be the best version of me and to continue to practice pure love and learn to be in my own power.

INTRODUCTION

As a child, waking up to the smell of coffee was a signal to me that work had begun. By five every morning, my mom would be downstairs cleaning chairs, tables, utensils and kitchenware in preparation for the day's customers. My mom and aunt shared the responsibility of running their family business, an old-fashioned Malaysian coffee shop. I grew up on the second floor above it with my parents, brothers, aunts, uncles, and my grandfather. There were four bedrooms, so you can imagine the limited space we had. I was used to sleeping on a mattress on the floor. I still remember falling to the floor the first time I slept on a regular bed! It was during my first trip to Canada. I was thirteen.

Despite growing up in such a small space, I enjoyed a fun and happy childhood. I was independent, an average student, and I enjoyed roaming around the town with neighborhood friends. I was a tomboy. I was shy and quiet. While still a pre-teen, I remembered struggling to look at myself in the mirror. I disliked being photographed. As I moved into my teen years, my self-esteem continued to crumble.

While taking a government proficiency test during the age of fifteen, I made a decision to change how I looked at the world. I decided to do better in school and to bring my grades up; from then on, things started to change. I can't recall what caused the change, all I remembered was I just had enough of being compared to others and that I was 'lesser' than others. Perhaps this is where I truly started my journey of discovering me. I studied hard for my exams, and I was one of the only two students in my school to earn seven 'A1's out of eight subjects.

From an early age, I knew that I wanted to go to school in the United States and then move to Canada. Quite a dream for a girl from the wrong side of the tracks! But why the United States? I might say that I watched too much television when I was young! Most of the pop stars and movie stars came from the States! The land of opportunity, as they say. Malaysia was a developing country, and it lacked many amazing products and services that were so abundant in the US. I couldn't stop dreaming about the possible lifestyle I could experience in the US. Of course, there was also the issue of freedom. As a Malaysian Chinese, I was treated like a second-class citizen in Malaysia. There were restrictions on speech, business opportunities and education. Too often, one's "skin" color determined whether or not one made it.

My dream to live in Canada was fueled by the first visit when I was thirteen. It was love at first sight! I remembered visiting a mall and being asked by someone if I needed assistance. No one ignored me because of my ethnicity. People were kind to me and didn't treat me like an inferior person. That was such a different experience for me! It was wonderful. It was freedom. I again felt 'enough'.

Eventually, I was able to go to the U.S. to study. I was

focused. I worked hard to get good grades, and my work paid off. To this day, I am proud that I earned my bachelor's degree in accounting from the University of Missouri-Columbia. It wasn't easy. I had to work in the dormitory and the university bookstore to pay my living expenses and my good grades assisted me in getting a few scholarships to pay for my tuition. Those experiences made me value my education all the more.

After reaching the milestone of college graduation, I pursued and earned a master's degree in business administration at the same university. My personal formula of hard work and dedication got me through the program as one of the top students in MIS. I then earned a PhD in Entrepreneurship. I created and delivered a fulfilling dissertation that focused on the "Personal Initiative" qualities of founding CEOs who successfully transitioned small and medium-sized enterprises into large corporations. This training and preparation formed the foundation of my current work and life.

My life has been described as dazzling by some who look from the outside in, so it seems. However, I've had my healthy share of trials and rude awakenings. I've experienced frightening financial debt, horrible disappointments and challenges in my personal relationship. I have felt alone, and I have felt sorry for myself. Early in these challenges, I felt victimized. I kept thinking it was always someone else making the bad times roll. I was always looking around for someone to blame. I was desperate!

Though I was half a million dollars in debt at the time, I listened to a strong intuitive voice that told me to attend a transformational training program. I am glad I listened! The seminar made me look at responsibility in a new way by introducing me to the concept that ownership is different to obligation and burden. Suddenly, I had a vision of the woman in the mirror, me, who was really responsible for my troubles. Together with this seminar and a year's coaches training program I completed, my life changed course for the better. This new direction not only empowered me, but it also gave me the strength and the opportunity to touch and empower the lives of others. I realized that loving myself and being authentic are the most powerful ways to live a life that leads to a the purest form of joy and peace.

I worked a lot on myself, and especially on breaking through limiting beliefs that stopped me from seeing the true essence of who I am. I experienced various modalities of clearing emotions, energy blocks and most importantly, learning to love myself. In the process, I began to dissolve obstacles that repeatedly held me back. These included the feeling that I was never good enough, that people didn't care about me and I didn't matter, that I was a horrible singer, that I was stupid and uncreative, that I was ugly. Blasting through these roadblocks allowed me to flow with the universe and begin to love myself.

Love myself—that was a project on its own! Once, I thought that the concept of loving oneself before loving others was a lot of baloney. Gradually though, I learned the truth of it. I began to see that it was essential for me to fill up my own tank before I could give to others. It's like imperiled flying. You must put on your own oxygen mask before putting one on a child. As a mother, I realized that when I felt too tired or overwhelmed, it was easier to turn my frustration and anger on my kids. They always knew when I was unhappy, and it hurt them. Yet, working with my shortcomings, I was able to begin to turn myself (and others) around. I discovered just how deeply we serve as models for our children. When we live in power and joy, they feel it and know they have the same gifts inside them. When we live powerless, as victims, they feel that, too, and often become just like us.

So when I began taking care of me, loving myself, and giving myself adequate downtime to do things I enjoyed, I began to feel happier. I was able to take on more responsibility and more work. I didn't get frustrated as easily. Loving myself more, I realized that I was becoming less judgmental of myself, and others, too. I saw that I was more creative and generating more positive experience for the people around me. That nagging, nasty voice in my head grew softer and softer, and the bully within me quieted down. More and more, I learned to detach myself from it. I discovered that that voice was not me, but the accumulated noise of past negative experiences.

I have gained a new perspective on what it means to live a happy life. At the core of my truth is this: there is no stronger power than that which comes from within; a kind of real power that springs from being able to trust and to love yourself as you bring out the joy from within and live a life of integrity. Acknowledging my mistakes gives me power, and being responsible gives me power. I need only to accomplish these two simple things and remember to stay true to be authentic and vulnerable. Acknowledgement and responsibility create trust and flow, freeing me to allow and accept what is. Accepting me for who I am and embracing all of me (the good, the bad and the ugly) with no judgments is true power. They also make generosity flow in and out. I can give and receive with grace and equanimity. This is what I called Power Love.

Do you wonder what it is to have a powerful life? Do you wonder what it looks like? Powerful living is being present in the moment, enjoying life and being fully empowered in your choices, actions and thoughts. Coming from the place of choice created by living a powerful life gives us the freedom to be our true selves, our integrated selves. We simply enjoy our life's journey. And this is what I'd like to share with you.

On each page of this book, I'll share my voice and insights gleaned from a life of pursuing happiness and growth. For years, friends and family members have expressed that they've been inspired by my journey, by the way I live my life, and so I'm excited to create and offer this book with the intention of supporting others striving to improve their lives. If sharing a part of myself, of my story, can do that, then I am deeply honored.

Let me say, too, that I am not a saint! I do not have all the answers. Like you, I am still on walking my path. I make mistakes. Too many times a day I am not present as I could be or would like to be. I have 'down' days, days when I feel I am not accomplishing all that I could. Yet, I can tell you that those days grow fewer and fewer, and that most of the time I live a life of peace, a life filled with joy and empowerment. In turn, I believe I can support you to feel grounded and present and to embrace your authentic, powerful self.

Today, I live in Canada (yes, I achieved that dream, too!) with my three lovely children. I'm an internationally bestselling author included in *Conversations That Make a Difference: Shift Your Beliefs To Get What You Want*. I direct several companies, including Dr. Annie Lim International, a company that integrates the Superlearning methodology in its programs. I established the L.I.F.E. Children Foundation with the intention to produce a positive change to the current educational system and provide underprivileged children with better educational opportunities. My children and I have travelled to Cambodia to support SSF, a foundation that supports sexually abused children. In 2013, I launched WEWORLD Network (Women Entrepreneurs World Network) and in 2015, Origin of Wisdom. I'm a certified ontological coach, licensed Reiki practitioner, Family Constellation practitioner, licensed Emotion Code practitioner, licensed Love Ambassador for Marci Shimoff programs, together with many others certified skills in NLP, DISC, and so on. I received the International Women's Day Outstanding Service Award from Women's Information Network, USA, and the Outstanding Contribution to Children Award from Voice of Nations. I've spoken and taught in the United States, Canada, Australia, Malaysia, the United Kingdom, Singapore and Thailand, and have shared the platform with the Queen from the Ga tribe in Accra, Ghana, HRM Queen Naa Tsotsoo Soyoo I, Nobel Peace Prize Laureate Dr. Shirin Ebadi, Oscar winning producer Barnet Bain, Datin Paduka Marina Mahathir, Jack Canfield, Arianna Huffington, Dame D. C. Cordova, Lisa Nichols and many others. Along the way, I've made time to tandem skydive from 10,000 feet, bungee jump and climbed Mount Kinabalu, the tallest mountain in Southeast Asia.

Given all of these activities, perhaps it's no surprise that I've met many people who think that I'm very, very busy, yet I don't feel that way. I feel alive! I enjoy every moment of what I do. I spend quality time with my children. I spend time connecting with myself. I spend time connecting with my partner (I prefer to call him my partner as the term husband comes with many expectations) and my friends. I have come to know and learned to trust the universe, which teaches that everything happens at the right time, at the right place and with the right people. In living this way, I am grateful for my life, for its simple daily joys.

I achieved this state of grace through diligent work. I work at maintaining it, even though, like you, I fall down a hundred times a day, and I get back up! So many of us, on some level, want more than we think we have. Some of us want the biggest home around. Some want to own nice cars, travel to faraway places and meet new and exciting people. Ultimately, though, from a deeper place, we all desire the same thing, which is to experience joy, peace, love, harmony and connection, and these alone grant us the power to live a life we can love. My intention is to share with you lessons that I have learned and support you to get there. I truly believe if I could do it, you could do it too as long as you are willing to practice and be open to learning about yourself in the process.

Before introducing to you the seven keys, let me say that these keys work hand in hand with each other and are in no particular order of practice. To get the best out of the practices suggested in this book, you may choose to read a chapter and work on the practices for a week or a month before proceeding and feel free to pick different chapters that call out to you.

So, let the journey begin.

KEY #1: BEING **PRESENT**

"The present moment is filled with joy and happiness. If you are attentive, you will see it." – Thich Nhat Hanh

What Is Present?

Nowadays, I live in the present most of the time. I spend very little time stuck in the past or the future, not that I disregard them! Oh, no. I work with my shadow on a daily basis, understanding obstacles and old patterns that have not served me well. My shadow is not just my outline on a wall. It's the voice and presence within me that generates fear, that suggests insidious ways I might fail. Our shadow is a rich field of exploration, and it's necessary to go there if we want to break through to an aware life in the present. It's also important to imagine the life we desire. I now live trusting and flowing with the universe knowing that everything I need shall be provided.

The universe guided me to the true meaning of being present in my life. I'd like to share a very short story about how I found Eckhart Tolle's *The Power of Now*, which taught me so much about this concept. One day, as I waited for my children, I wandered around in a bookstore, and I felt something calling amidst the sea of books. I was drawn to a certain aisle and shelf, and there, face-out, was *The Power of Now*. When one is ready, one is called to what one needs. My fingers and hands literally tingled as I picked it up and thumbed through its pages. I didn't know it then, but Tolle's words would broaden my perspective on living life in the present.

Often, many of us miss the present moment; we do not accept its gift and savor it. At that moment, we forget to experience fully what we're doing. Sometimes when we're chatting, thinking or listening to music while we eat, we miss an opportunity to engage with someone else; we don't really tune in to the wisdom of our thoughts, we allow the music to rush past us rather than enter us, and we chew and swallow but do not taste or be thankful for the plant or animal providing sustenance, or the many people responsible for bringing it to our table. Being present means being mindful of every moment we're alive. It's a state of pure peace, joy, love and freedom.

The present is also a safe vessel for our shadows, their sadness, anger and fears. Being in the present moment quiets the rumbling thoughts and chatter in our heads and unveils the clear consciousness of our present circumstances. A practice of being in the present moment empowers one with the *ability to be with*. Here is an example. I used to get angry when my children cried and whined for too long, then I would feel guilty. There was no win in this dynamic for my children or me. I have learned that I needed to be with my own pain and hurt, with my own beliefs of what crying means to me, what I was told about it when I was growing up and how it affects me and once I got that, I was able to be with my kids when they cried. This precious skill allows us to work through our fears, anxieties and the unhelpful opinions of others. As a result, we gain the strength to *accept* circumstances as they are instead of trying to change the results to the outcomes we think we'd prefer (which is driven very much by our beliefs). This is a practice in surrender and trust in life's inherent goodness. This is a practice of submitting to the great mystery of life and believing that the key to satisfaction and happiness can be found in one place, and one place only—within.

There was a time when I infrequently could fully enjoy anything in life. Whether it be the company of those who surrounded me, or the activities I participated in, they all lacked sparkles. They felt mundane before I learned to live in the present. I recognized this situation, yet I spent way too much time looking at others for the cause of my ennui. I thought it had to be someone else's fault, that others were somehow holding me back from achieving my goals and satisfying my desires. How foolish of me! At that point in my life, I felt as if I was mindlessly driving a car towards an unknown destination. When I arrived, all I could say was, "Oh, we're here…" and nothing more. The poet Robert Penn Warren wrote, "You are alone with the alone, and it is his move." That's how I felt. Somehow, I missed the beauty of the journey. I did not feel the breeze, hear the music, drink in the scenery, or tune in to the people I met along the way.

What was the point? Then I realized that I'd been allowing the stories of my past to run my life. What good did it do to think that the world was so mean to me? What good did it do to ask over and over again, "what have I done?" I took a long time before I realized that only I was actually the one who was attached to each and every one of the situations that had occurred in my life and were holding me back. Suddenly, I woke up to the realization that they were all in the past. There was nothing I could do about them now! Nothing except acknowledging them and let them go. I realized that it is better to embrace them and accept them as lessons learned along this wonderful path I was on.

Before that breakthrough moment, I'd invent stories about the future, too. Of course, they were based on fear, because I believed that things would inevitably turn out badly for me. So, I would waste even more time planning ways to avoid future negative outcomes. Talk about being trapped in your own head! Only after my revelation was I able to see that I could no longer proceed from a place of fear if I wanted to move closer towards a happier, more powerful life. I chose to live from love.

Connection Is Essential

Over the years, I've learned to recognize this very same painful process in the lives of the individuals I've met and worked with around the globe. Their use of words in the past or future tenses often clue me in on where they actually are at the moment. Though it is difficult to describe at times, there are instances when I connect with others and they're just not there. A strong disconnection results when they fail to meet my gaze. When we do not look at each other, we do not fully receive and hear each other. Connection is essential if we intend to be awake and present. It is important to pay attention to expressions and gestures and to look deeply into each other's eyes.

Until you break through your own obstacles, you will miss out on so much in life. Living in a disappointing past and frightening future robs you of the wonderful today you can spend with your family, colleagues, partner, children and friends. You must, and you can, break free of the straitjacket of the victim profile. You can replace the negative programming you've inherited with positive programming, and you can create stories and listen to the stories of others in new, self-soothing ways. You can enjoy being in the moment, being alive and present. It takes you to choose consciously to be here right now and to be fully connected to yourself and savor the moment.

For instance, I have had many challenges in my relationship with my partner; I realized that many of our arguments arose because we were stuck in the past. Things I had done, and he had done, became triggers for both of us. Later, as I became more conscious of my thoughts, I practiced coming from the present, the very moment that I have with each new breath. Now, I can acknowledge him for who he is in the moment; I can honor his wholeness and completion. When I express my love for him, I choose to see him in the moment rather than in some past scenario where I perceived he was wronging or hurting me. This has made every moment special and precious. I now live daily built on this lesson and practice being present with everything and everyone in my life.

It is truly amazing to me how being present in the moment allows me to connect with others on so many deeper levels. Today, I am able to listen with all my being, and give my undivided attention to what I see and feel. This allows me to savor each and every minute of my experience! My life has dramatically changed for the better because I am fully engaged and filled with clarity, joy and peace. The same can be true for you!

Living in the present has empowered me in so many positive ways. Today, my family and friends are happier with the quality of the relationships we share. If you asked them, they would tell you that they feel listened to and acknowledged every time I show up for them. They would also say that they appreciate the deep sense of love and support that I am able to give when I'm with them.

More than anything, being present in my life supports and strengthens the relationship that I share with each of my children. I used to be with them physically, but my mind would often drift away to work or grocery shopping or car maintenance—all of the daily busywork that so many parents must deal with in our world. But now, it feels wonderful to enjoy my children for who they really are as young individuals. Being able to play with them in the fullness of my being is priceless. By calling on all of my senses, by playing with them as a child, I tap in to a deep sense of joy as their mother.

The power to be present in the moment resides in each of us. It's a matter of choice. Each of us is granted the freedom to choose who we want to be and what we want to do in any given moment. If you remember just one thing, let it be this: every moment in your life is a choice that only you can make. So it is, so it will be.

Practices

Learning to be present in your life is easy. However, we all need a lot of practice in order to perfect its application in daily life. As I've often said, we're all programmed one way or another to master the art of being or not being in the moment. To support you in this process, I'd like to support you as you advance from the past you can't change and a future you might be worrying about. Here are some simple ways to start living in the present today.

Practice #1: *Become Aware Of Your Presence*

Awareness is always the first step in finding solutions and answers. However, when it comes to being mindful of our presence in the moment, it is not an easy task in the beginning. It takes time and effort to recognize when we are not truly immersing ourselves in the present. Gaining consciousness needs practice and patience to master it. Keep in mind that it is only through knowing yourself and your thoughts that you become empowered with the capacity to redirect them.

One helpful exercise is writing down your observations in a small notebook you can easily carry around with you. Take a walk. Keep your eyes on the horizon rather than looking down at your feet. This will expand your thoughts and calm your mind while softening the din of too much internal chatter. As you walk, be with the plants you encounter. Smell them, look at their beauty, touch them, and enjoy each moment with them. When you see someone else, notice what he or she is wearing. What does their body language tell you? How do you feel when you look at this person? This attention to detail will be very helpful when applying the second centering method – Practice #2 Breathe.

Allowing the mind to become curious like a newborn child is so important. Take in your experiences and surroundings as if you've never heard, smelled, tasted or seen them before. Feel a sense of wonder in your experience.

Practice #2: *Breathe*

Breathing is one of the natural ways the body brings

new energy into our system. Concentrating on the breath is one of the easiest ways to refocus ourselves when we start to drift away and entertain the pains of the past or our worries for the future.

As you inhale and exhale new life into your body, visualize your heart. Make it the center of your presence. After that, say out loud and with conviction: I am here…I am present.

This two-step centering method has never failed to bring me back to where I ought to be as it reminds me of the wonderful present or gift of the moment I have at that time. This is simple, yes, yet oh so effective. Give it a go!

Practice #3: *Track Communication*

A tool we can use to observe how often we live in the past, present or future is to consciously track our communication. Draw a timeline with two axis—horizontal axis represents time movement, and vertical axis represents the past, present and future. As you speak, notice the words you use. If you are referencing the past, you will move the pencil downwards; if you speak in the present, you will draw a straight line; if you speak in the future, your line will move up. This gives you an opportunity to observe your thought process, to practice speaking from the present. This will retrain your mind to think in the present moment.

Practice #4: *Play With Children*

Children are awesome at this! In her pure innocence my daughter, Joy, reminds me to be in the moment when she says, "Mommy, put down your phone and play with me."

Those simple words really jolt me into the present moment, which is offering me the precious opportunity to be with my daughter in a meaningful way.

So, commit to play with children. If you don't have kids of your own, go visit your friends' children or your nephews or nieces. Learn to be with them. Observe them. You will learn so much about being present in the moment from them.

Practice #5: *Eat Mindfully*

When its time for you to enjoy your wondrous meal, instead of focusing on your conversations or watching television, taste every morsel of your food. Eat slowly. Taste the food and the texture. Enjoy the aroma. Be mindful of the smell of the food. Be mindful of your body whether you had enough or you are present to your hunger. By practicing mindful eating, you become present to yourself and your food.

Practice #6: *Listen With Your Presence*

Pay attention to how you listen to someone. Are you listening to what is said, or are you blocking it with your preconceived ideas about the conversation? This is an excellent beginning for an awareness practice. With awareness comes clarity. With clarity comes power.

Practice #7: *Meditate*

Like you, many years of multitasking, worry, and holding on to past wounds led me far away from the ability to rest easy in the present moment. We've all been trained to listen to the voices in our heads, the voices telling us that each and every word they utter is an important part of whom we are and who we ought to be. Trouble is, some of those voices really just lead us back to a blocked past, or they make us leap ahead to live in an imaginary future fraught with uncertainty and anxiety. These chatters can go on and on and on like the energizer bunny and we get so caught up with the voices that we forget to be present. We are faced with a choice: *be present or absent in our now*.

Meditation will help you turn down the volume of these voices that do not serve you well. Meditating to be present is basically just observing your breathing and noticing every thought that is coming and making no judgment and let it go and come back to observing your breathing. It could be as simple as this or you could google and find some meditation scripts that support you in getting present.

Practice #8: *Speak Or Write What's On Your Mind To Get Present*

Another practice is to just speak what is on your mind. No editing or correction, just allow whatever wants to be said and say it. And if you are much more comfortable with writing, write it down. This will allow you to just get everything that is on your mind out and allow you to be fully present again.

I also use a tool with many of the teams I work with. This tool is a very simple tool called "What I Am Present To Is…" So basically it is to invite the individual to say whatever is on her or his mind in that particular moment– it could be the lunch they just ate, or they are thinking of whether or not they turned the stove off at home, and so on.

This supports the individual to say whatever is in one's thoughts and then to refocus one's attention to the meeting.

KEY #2: REMEMBER TO **PLAY**

"We are never more fully alive, more completely ourselves, or more deeply engrossed in anything, than when we are at play." – Charles E. Schaefer

Play Like You Never Played Before

When was the last time you enjoyed a hearty laugh? When was the last time you didn't pass judgment on anything or anyone else? How long has it been since you could truly say that you were having fun, and when was the last time you felt like a child?

It's healthy for you to play with children, and it's healthy to feel like a child, too. We all carry our inner child inside of us, and that divine being clamors for comfort and attention. Your inner child can cling to you, ball up its fists and throw a tantrum or lie almost comatose deep inside your core. Whether you are paying attention to her or him or not, the child is always present. Developing easy access to your inner child is absolutely essential if you want to be awake in the moment. Your inner child gifts you with more balance and is an affectionate inner ally who will support you in anything you do.

Seeing children play and enjoying themselves is just an amazing sight! They don't dwell on the past or fret about the future. They don't obsess over the food they'll eat or when they'll eat it. Most children are involved in their immediate play activities, and they quickly forget the inevitable petty quarrels that erupt. Think about it. Usually, two children who get into a scrap are playing together in a matter of minutes.

Children are truly miraculous. Unlike many adults, young ones possess the awakening ability to let things go. They don't hold on to negative feelings, and most are incapable of holding grudges. They're free from the obsession with being right, and they're immune to the resentment that often comes of those desires. They are able to have fun and *just be*. Children are open, vulnerable and forgiving, and oh, how they laugh!

So, I ask you—if you had the time and freedom, would you allow yourself to play and be as carefree as the child you once were? In this chapter, we'll explore the process of nurturing your inner child, which will allow fun to take over your lives. I want to share my own story of how I found my path to fun, and suggest ways that you can find your path, too.

In the *Introduction*, I mentioned that I did not come from a well-to-do family, but this never stopped us from striving to realize our dreams. With hard work and intense focus which I learned from my parents, I was able to complete my bachelor's degree in accounting with honors at the University of Missouri-Columbia, and eventually relocated to Canada. The lessons of my childhood taught me to aspire to things that are greater than myself. I learned that all of them were attainable. This belief gave birth to my dream of a better life not only for myself but also for my parents and our family.

As soon as I completed college, I focused on building a career that would earn enough income to support my dream of a better life. For a time, I fell into a familiar trap that many of you will recognize. Over time, I realized that my lifestyle was changing. The way I was living demanded more money, and before I knew it, I was locked into a mindset in which I believed that I needed to work more and more in order to sustain my lifestyle and become even more successful.

As I focused on success and the creation of wealth, I convinced myself that I had to sacrifice activities I loved— riding horses, going out with friends, watching movies, doing things I love. After all, these could be seen as frivolous expenses or just plain money drains. But doing away with the horseback riding and going out with friends depleted my energy. Suddenly, I felt more exhausted than I ever had in my life. I couldn't help but feel like a car running on empty but still sputtering to reach its destination. What was wrong with successful me?

As I struggled with this dilemma, my training to become a certified coach proved to be my lifeline. Through that rich experience, I realized that I had been putting the needs of everyone else above my own. I stopped paying for activities that nurtured me emotionally, physically and spiritually, and instead directed that income to the needs of my children. While that may appear to be admirable, the truth is it did not make me a better mother. I wasn't as happy as I'd once been, and I slid into resentment and frustration. Children are naturally empathetic. Don't think for a moment that they aren't affected by their parents' moods.

I learned this, and I suffered because what I was doing was not in line with the desires of my inner child, who genuinely loved me and wanted to come out and play. In time, I opened my eyes and saw that I needed to take better care of myself, and my inner child. And guess what happened? The moment I started doing that, I came alive and felt the desire to play and have fun again. I was able to say that I truly felt my resentment and anger dissolving and releasing their grip on me. I no longer felt like their prisoner. Giving myself permission to play again transformed me into who I really am: the creative and funny Annie who has a big heart to share with the world.

Play Intentionally

But just what *is* conscious play? It's as simple as this: having fun in the moment. It's about being able to see and fully engage in everything you do. Being conscious means that you are clear about your intentions to have fun in the moment. Laughter and fun heal! Keeping this perspective truly turns every moment into a fun and experimental adventure that can and will enrich your life.

When I started experiencing the benefit of play, I began exploring more into conscious play and came to learn about a book by Stuart Brown, M.D., *Play: How It Shapes the Brain, Opens the Imagination, and Invigorates the Soul.* Dr. Brown talks about how play is important to renewing our natural sense of optimism and opens us up to new possibilities. He found that remembering what play is all about and making it part of our daily lives are probably the most important factors in being a fulfilled human being.

The ability to play is critical not only to being happy, but also to sustaining social relationships and being a creative, innovative person. He shared how he had found evidence that happier and healthier people use play in all their lives; they become more productive, better parents and actually get sick less frequently. He also found how play increases harmony and effectiveness in relationships. So, it is not just an idea, it is actually scientific.

In order to get to this life-changing state, there are two misconceptions about play that I want to address.

First, having fun has nothing to do with going on a drinking spree, partying all night or taking illegal drugs. These addictive behaviors are defense mechanisms that temporarily cloud over the pain and unresolved issues in our lives. Please consider that these behaviors will not bring us any closer to the purest form of play. With that said, never confuse these temporary pleasures with the sustainable joy that authentic play offers.

The second thing I would like you to remember about play is this: there is no age limit! I know that many of us intentionally restrain ourselves from playing because it is not right or perhaps it's inappropriate. But let me tell you, each and every one of us has an inner child that needs to be nurtured and loved. When you confine and shut down your inner child, you are literally increasing toxicity in your body. Nothing ages you faster than taking yourself too seriously and forgetting to laugh and play. If you want evidence of this, think of the people you know. Notice the differences between those who play and laugh, and those who are deadly serious and decidedly un-fun.

Maybe you can write these differences down for easier comparison. I think you'll see, and once you see, you'll decide you'd much rather be with someone who laughs and plays. Those are the people who enjoy life and have fun. So, set your inner child free by allowing play and fun to enter your life today.

I love water gun fights. And today, I enjoy it more when I play it with my children. It's not easy to see yourself as a 10-year old when you're a full grown adult with a list of responsibilities that remind you of it. But when I have water gun fights with my little ones, I just tell myself that I have to let go of thoughts that it is not okay to play as an adult. I have to drop the façade of having to look and behave like an adult. I need to let go of any judgment or fear of being criticized by others, especially the judgment of how silly, embarrassing or inappropriate it is. This has been my first step in experiencing a deep kind of joy when I play with my children.

Yes, I do get soaked – but they get soaked too. It's just fun and I don't care how I look before or after the game. I don't even think of what could possibly happen 5 minutes after we're done, let alone what might happen in a year or two. All that matters is that I'm present in the moment and playing with my children. We're happy and that's all there is to it.

Remember that having fun begins with doing things that you enjoy the most. Never be afraid to let yourself go in order to experience the real meaning of fun in your life.

Choose Fun

Having fun is a choice. You can resolve to be truly happy now, a second later, a minute or even a week later. The choice is up to you. Keep in mind that you always have a choice.

Every second and every breath you take ends as soon as it is over. Seize every moment and think of play as being you and being present in the moment. Harnessing the power of play in your life empowers you to let go of negative energies as it nourishes your inner child. Release your power within and embrace the true meaning of fun in your life. Here are some helpful practices for you.

Practices

Practice #1: *Go To The Playground*

Visit a playground. Sit on one of the benches and observe the children playing. Maybe you can bring along a child from your family. Whether you go with a child or not, go! Take a notebook, too, and jot down your feelings, thoughts and observations. Perhaps you'll even feel like getting up to participate. Good! Push a child on a swing. Swing on the monkey bars. Make a fortress in the sandbox. Play, and soon, you'll find yourself laughing.

Practice #2: *Join A Laughter Club*

Find a laughter club and attend a meeting. Laughter clubs began in Sweden and have spread around the world. What is a laughter club? Well, it's just what it sounds like. A group of diverse people gets together and laughs. They do loud guffaws, short, little laughs, gulping laughs, and big, boisterous laughs. They do any laughs the attendees can think of. After half an hour, you will be standing in a room filled with happy, in-the-moment people, and you will be one of them! If you can't find a laughter club in your area, consider starting one. Laughter is a terrific healer, and it's free!

Practice #3: *Be Silly*

Commit to doing one silly thing a day. Make this part of your daily spiritual practice. Wear a funny hat around for a few minutes. Put on mismatched socks. Make silly faces in the mirror, or talk in a goofy voice. And when the spirit moves you, throw back your head and laugh!

Practice #4: *Do Something You Enjoyed Playing When You Were A Child*

Pick something you liked to do as a child and invite some friends to share the activity with you. For instance, flying a kite. Nothing is more fun than kite flying. Again, you may up the ante and send your fun-o-meter spinning wildly round and round if you fly a kite with a child. Alone or with someone, fly a kite. You will catch yourself smiling, feeling happy and in the present moment. You'll laugh, too, and not just at the wonderful notion that there you are, a grown-up with a busy schedule, taking time off to stand in a park or field or on a beach and fly a kite.

Write down a list of what you loved to play when you were young and start doing them again.

Here are some additional practices you might take on! And keep adding on activities or games to the list.

1. Singing lessons.
2. Sign up for salsa classes.
3. Skydiving.

4. Go out with friends.
5. Play any sports you love.
6. Play bubbles – yep, you read it right – bubbles!
7. Run across the field. Now you add a few!
8. _____
9. _____
10. _____

Practice #5: *Fun Time With Mirror*

Write down a brief story about anything you like. It might be a story about something that happened to you at work today, or it could be about something you did with a close friend or loved one. Write the story, then stand before a mirror and read it aloud. Do this a couple of times. Pay attention to your voice. How does it sound to you? Are you going slowly enough to enunciate well and give added meaning to certain words and moments? Also, pay attention to your facial expressions and your body. Are you too stiff? Are you hiding emotion? Work on these as you re-read your story. Finally, put down your written pages and tell the story without the aid of notes or a script. Just tell it. If you feel yourself stopping or getting stuck, make something up and keep going! Or start over.

Remember, this is play! Have fun. Be kind to yourself, and be interested in yourself! You can do this!

Practice #6: *Learn A New Art Or Skill*

Learn something new, have fun with it, go with the lens of play. For example, if you love to dance, go dancing! If you think of yourself as not much of a dancer, take the courageous step to become one! You might begin in your own home. Put on music you love, music that speaks to you on a deep, personal level. Stand in the center of the room, and when you feel the urge, just start moving. Dance your truth! There's no one watching you. Fight through your self-consciousness and move. You may discover the delicious sensations that attend your moving body. Size doesn't matter! Whether you're large or small, tall or short, repeat to yourself the truth that you are beautiful. You are!

Perhaps then you may want to take the next step. Do a little research in your area and contact a dance instructor. You may opt for private or group lessons. Either one will work. It doesn't matter what kind of dancing you learn. All are good! Just try it. You'll find a reservoir of self-confidence and self-love within as you begin to pay attention to your blessed body in motion. You'll discover personal freedom, and you'll find yourself zeroing in on your inner child just having fun and playing.

KEY #3: **PASSIONATELY** CURIOUS

"I have no special talents. I am only passionately curious."
– Albert Einstein

Passion Is A Big Word Or Is It Not

When you hear the word, Passion, what comes to your mind?

I have heard many people say *I don't know what my passion is* or *I don't know where to start to realize it and release it*. In all my experience, one of the most popular questions people young and old want an answer to is this: *How do I find my passion?* Do you have the same question?

In this chapter, join me as we explore your passion. If our subject appears to be a little too abstract to absorb in a span of a few pages, it's okay; I am here to support you through this journey of discovering your passion that announces itself to the world, that tells everyone who you really are. That's what passion is: a strong intense emotion of desire and aliveness; a creative energy within you that can't wait to be expressed.

Let me begin by telling you something that may startle you in its simplicity. Knowing your passion is as easy as answering one question: if you had all the money and time in the world today, what would you do with them? Would you buy more clothes, jewelry, appliances and cars? Perhaps you'd quit your job, or travel around the world. Would you invest it? Would you start your own business? Would you give it to your children, or give it away to strangers?

Any or all of these things might make you feel good for a time, but would they truly satisfy your passion? Would you be able to look at any of them and say, yes, this is exactly who I am in the world? If you're doubtful, you're wise to feel that way. Products, travel and even gifting others exist outside you, while your passion bubbles up and springs from within. Yet, before your passion can benefit others, it has to be recognized and embraced by you. It has to feel nurtured. Only through sitting and walking with your shadow can you seek within yourself and discover your true passion. I know what you're thinking! Easier said then done. And yet, the process really is easier than you think!

So many of us manage to make this process of finding our passion more *complicated* than it actually needs to be. You may have been living for a long time now with the belief that the only way to achieve real results in your search for passion is to go down the most difficult path you can find. For many, struggle and suffering are signs that you're paying your dues. But that process, especially when you're seeking your passion, doesn't always justify the authenticity of what you discover. More often than not, this way of thinking leads you farther away from the passion that you've intuitively carried along with you since you were born.

Throughout this book, and hopefully after it, I'd like you to remember that your passion is not complicated and too big. It's attainable. It's right there waiting for you. This truth applies to both the passion itself and the journey towards the discovery of it. Keep in mind that anything having to do with passion need not be a grueling obstacle course.

Follow Your Passion

My life journey, to this point, has taught me that human passion is *dynamic* and *fluid*. Our love of activities, people, circumstances, noble callings or whatever it is that fills our hearts with joy can change. It can also grow stronger or waste away over time with no regret. It's certain, though, that our passion fuels our drive towards Presence.

If we answer the question, "What do you love to do in your life?" by saying that we love to cook and we would do it no matter how others stop us and we'd continue to persist, then that is our passion. If we adore stamp collecting, that is our passion. Passion is neither positive nor negative; it's powerful. It's up to each of us to choose and develop passion that is good for us and beneficial to others.

For passionately living people, their passion is the first thing that comes to mind when they wake up in the morning. They don't spend a lot of time thinking about it. They wake up feeling eager, inspired and raring to go. Getting out of bed is fun! They feel energized and empowered because they are alive and free to pursue their passion. Anything or anyone may make them feel this way. That's what sets your passion apart from anything else in your life—its ability to inspire you even when you're feeling the duress of tremendous difficulties. That which you love so much will never feel burdensome to you.

I don't mean to imply that finding your passion is always easy. It takes commitment. It takes work—happy work. For instance, I spent thirty years of my life searching for my passion before I discovered my deep love of training and mentoring. I also discovered that, just like you, I can have and hold multiple passions. Today, I also love being an entrepreneur. I even discovered while writing this book that another passion of mine is starting businesses. Speaking before a crowd is a passion I've also recognized and developed. Being blessed with opportunities to inspire others and encourage them to live their lives to the fullest gives me a deep sense of fulfillment that never ends.

I have come to learn that we can be multi-passionate, as Marie Forleo calls it. My daughter, Joy and my son Jordan love to talk about what they want to grow up to be. Jordan enjoys baking, drawing, acting and singing and playing video games – so whenever I ask, what do you want to be when you grow up? He will say – "well, I am going to be a world class chef owning my own restaurant, be an artist and also an actor." In his mind, it's not I am going to be a chef and that's it. Joy has now come to embrace that and she says she is going to be a dancer, singer, actor, youtuber, chef like Jordan and sometimes Ninja!

When I began conducting trainings to support individuals develop their skills and sharpen their focus, I was shy and preferred to remain behind the scene as much as possible. Coordinating events and making sure that the programs ran smoothly were two things I really loved doing. But over time, one of my friends and business partner, Allan, was persistent in encouraging me to step up and conduct the trainings myself. This simple boost paved the way for discovering my passion for training and coaching.

Little did I know that the small role I played in conducting training in my first boot camp would usher in a tremendous change in my life. Seeing the participants grow and begin to realize their potential inspired me so much! From that moment on, I could see that there were endless possibilities and opportunities for all participants. It was as if I could peer into every heart in the room, and what I found there was limitless talent. Moving forward one step at a time, I got more deeply involved in training and eventually became a full-fledged trainer. Now I delight in my diverse focus on personal development, leadership, team-building and spiritual teachings.

In addition to my passion for supporting others as they realize their full potential and awakening to live in the present moment, my family is also my passion. Spending time with and talking about my children and parents have always been inspiring experiences, to the point of giving me goose bumps! In this way, I feel light and fully connected to the Great Spirit that is my Higher Power. The inspiration that springs from my passion for my family never fails to fill me up with an indescribable reserve of positive energy that continually flows in abundance.

There are two big things that can get in your way. These don't just get in your way. They can lock you down in solitary confinement and make you feel there's no escape and no path to your freedom.

Where We Get Caught

Money and time are two obstacles that make the simplicity of finding your passion a blur. Countless times, we measure our passion by attaching monetary value to it, and if things don't happen fast enough, we tend to believe that we're heading in the wrong direction. It's easy to lose focus this way. For instance, there are many components involved in creating and growing a business for profit.

Keep in mind that that there are challenges in every business pursuit. Being passionate about your business and the goals you intend to reach are what get you through the tough times and overcome obstacles. It may sound like a cliché, but too many business owners underestimate the role that passion plays in the success not only of their business, but in their lives in general. While I was doing my Ph.D., I asked Founding CEOs of leading growth companies to name their three secret ingredients to success; without fail, most of them mentioned passion as one of the three. I'd like you to remember that life is not about the money you make or the time you spend earning it. *Life is about life itself.* It is about the quality moments we share with each other.

So, are you thinking, "What does she mean that life is about life itself? Is she being cryptic? Is she being simplistic about this subject?"

Well, I'd like you to pause for a moment to experience the true meaning of life. Just breathe and consciously notice your breath as you inhale and exhale. That is your life. Being in the moment to experience and feel is life itself. It's a simple fact in our life journey that many of us tend to complicate it. Life is about living every minute as if it were your last. Life is about being, which springs from every individual's pure existence, unique beauty, wisdom and creativity.

Ask The Right Questions

Write it in your heart that we were all created equal. There is no need to entertain the constant pressure to measure up to others or become better than someone else. When you slip into this thinking, please ask yourself: To whom or what am I comparing myself? When will I know that I've achieved enough? And, what is enough? Chances are you'll never come up with a sound answer because each one of us is one of a kind that can't be truly matched by or compared to another. There's an old saying that sometimes we can't seem to answer a question because it's the wrong question!

There is no need to pursue a never-ending chase for perceived better or greater things in life. That's a fool's road, and it need not be yours. Only one question in life is worth asking: What brings you joy? Your passion will always be a self-generating life force that releases an authentic joy from within. This is the power of passion in your life. You are willing to do whatever it takes. Harness it to transform the way you live and live a life you love.

Practices

Practice #1: *Notice What Brings You Joy*

Do this exercise. Keep your little notebook beside you for one day. In it, jot down the people, scenes and things that give you joy. This will only take a few seconds each time! Write them down, and in a quiet moment at the end of the day, review your list. How do they connect in you? How do you feel? The way you feel will tell you a lot about your passion. You may feel so good, you'll want to do this exercise for several days. Go ahead! The discoveries are all your own, and the more you learn about your passion— where it resides in you, where it wants expression—will only enrich and empower your precious life.

Practice #2: *What Did You Enjoy Doing When You Were A Child*

Revisit your childhood and write down what you loved to do when you were a child. Do you still enjoy doing them now?

Practice #3: *Who Do You Admire And/Or Love?*

Make a list of individuals you admire and/or love. What do they possess or what are they doing that you like so much? Is it the profession they are in? List the talent they have? This may give you a clue to your own passion.

Practice #4: *What Do You Spend Time Reading?*

Make a list of books you read. What topics are they? Business, Sports, Animals, Peace, Spirituality and be more specific. What about business that interests you? Is it in the area of finance, or marketing or sales? For sports, is it the techniques, teaching the techniques, is it basketball, is it football? For peace, is your interest in creating peace in the world through ending poverty, providing water? Keep generating the list and please do not edit whatever comes to your mind. You might be surprised what you might discover.

Practice #5: *Challenging Times*

Write down a list of the things that you have continued to pursue despite facing challenges after challenges? This might give you some insight into what you are passionate about.

Practice #6: *Ask Others*

List about 10 people who are in your life that you are close to, people you love to hang out with and whose company you enjoy. Ask them what they think you love to do? Ask them what you talk about always and frequently with enthusiasm?

Practice #7: *Ask Yourself Some of These Questions*

1. What activities make you lose track of time?
2. If you had to teach something, what would you teach?
3. What are you naturally good at? (Skills, abilities, gifts etc.)

KEY #4: LIVING AND BEING ON **PURPOSE**

"There is no greater gift you can give or receive than to honor your calling. It is why you where born and how you become most truly alive." – Oprah Winfrey

"The two most important days in life are the day you are born and the day you discover the reason why." – Mark Twain

Knowing Your Purpose

So many questions! Yet, this is a big one. Once we connect with our inner passion, many of us feel the desire to reach out to others, to share what we've learned, and to create meaningful work we can do with purpose. It took me quite awhile to figure this one out—my purpose—but I can happily say that I am consistently living my passion and purpose today.

Discovering the real essence of my life has been a wonderful and fulfilling journey that opened one door after another. It led me to a path of self-discovery, and in this chapter, I invite you to walk with me as I revisit a truly enriching process in my life.

Like a lot people, I used to think that my life purpose was a destination rather than a journey, that creating a meaningful life meant having one significant purpose to live out as long as I live. To me, a life of purpose meant doing something that satisfied the bigger picture, the one beyond Annie and her personal sphere.

Discovering Your Path

Have you ever asked: *Where is my life headed? Where is it going?*

Some of us have a clear direction when we choose the path we will follow. Some of us cling to religion, which teaches us all about heaven and hell after this life, and the way we must walk our paths to achieve one and avoid the other. Religion offers a ready-made structure for one's search, but many others among us do not find this compatible with their inner life force. They continue to search for the meaning of their existence, and often they're confused about who they really are and what they want to accomplish.

The process of discovering one's purpose in life can be intimidating, and it can be especially so for those of us who lack a clear sense of direction. Becoming aligned with your path and sense of direction allows you to make decisions from a foundation of purpose, which gathers intentions and focus, and aids you as you take each step. In my life, I've discovered this foundation—this place of purpose—and I've seen how it positively affects not only our relationships, but every aspect of our lives.

After experiencing Buckminster Fuller and his concept of precession and adding value, I had a clearer idea of what my purpose was here on earth, the real essence of my existence. Buckminster Fuller says that we may not know our 'true' purpose, some of us may get to see a glimpse of it or yes some of us may discover it. What is more important is what we create while we are working towards our goals in life. He calls this concept, Precession. The Law of Precession simply states that for every action we take there will be a side effect arising at 90 degrees to the line of our action.

Think about honey bees. They spend their lives flying from flower to flower to collect nectar to make honey. They 'think' that's their purpose, but their true (and much larger) purpose is to pollinate the flowers. This is the Law of Precession - the effect of bodies in motion on other bodies in motion. Buckminster Fuller's theory says that our job was not to make money. It was to add value to others. We must simply be in motion, do something, and it will in turns create a precessional effect. It doesn't really matter what the doing is, as long as it is positive. That's our 'true' purpose.

So no matter where you are right now, what circumstances you are in, as long as you are willing to be in motion, you are on purpose. Say, if you are now jobless and are at your parents' home, know that you being in motion like doing laundry, cooking for them and yourself; the precessional effect is that you and your parents will have clean clothes which might probably make you and them feel better, you cooking them an awesome meal and having the opportunity to enjoy great company is how you are adding value which is your 'true' purpose for now! I can go on with many different scenarios. Remember to focus on adding value and you are on purpose.

Thanks to that experience at the seminar, I know that I live to inspire others. Seeing others discover their true selves has become my passion and that is how I can add value. This exhilarating love strengthened my desire to inspire and support one billion people in this lifetime on their own journeys of self-discovery. My mission is to be and do all I can to support them to live to their full potential and to embrace who they are fully. It might seem impossible and all too random since I just plucked that number out in the air, but I trust that the universe will guide me through making the desires of my heart a reality. Although I might not know the 'true' purpose, knowing that I have made a positive impact in their lives serves my well-being and my purpose here on earth.

Developing Your Purpose From Within

As my desire to become a trainer took shape, I began looking for programs that would support me in becoming a great one. At the time, I remember feeling so impatient! I wanted to get moving, but my patience and discipline paid off. I chose to participate in the Instructor Training Program before pursuing a training path with the *Money and You* program. This decision brought new meaning, purpose and focus to my life.

Over the course of twelve months, I thoroughly learned the course work and chose some of the pieces I would need to present. The first piece I was to present was about Self Mastery. I was so into the materials! They literally became part of my daily life. They changed how I felt and thought about people and things. They added rich new layers to my comprehension, and they increased and sharpened my empathy, my ability to listen and connect deeply with others. I began to look at my own life with a softer critical focus that was still rigorous. My self-confidence grew, as did my acceptance, both of others and myself. As I learned more about mastery, I especially applied my knowledge to the areas in which I wanted to improve, including teaching, public speaking and business management.

During the training program, I found the courage to offer presentations at previews, and I gained valuable feedback that improved my performance and pointed me in the right direction towards making greater improvements. For instance, I knew I possessed a soft voice, so I needed to learn to project it better if I ever intended to achieve my goals. I also learned that the stiffness of my body hindered me from being fully present when I was playing games, which was something we would do when asked to facilitate programs. The third thing I really needed to work on was the art of telling a story. My storytelling skills weren't what they needed to be, and I practiced and practiced to improve myself in this area too.

And guess what? I began taking singing lessons to learn how to project my voice. I also signed on for dance lessons, which trained my body to be more natural and present in the moment, and taught my ego not to get in my way! I even joined an acting class in my never-ending quest to become a better trainer.

For most of my life to that point, I'd always believed that I couldn't sing. This false and negative belief dated from my childhood when I took piano lessons. When I was 8 years old, one of my piano teachers told me that I couldn't sing, that my voice was too small, and I believed her! For many years, I simply accepted what that teacher told me, and oh, how it held me back! We have to be careful with the advice we get and the pronouncements that others make about us. Some are not at all helpful. They can be wrong, and they can establish a pattern of self-criticism that serves only to get in our way as we seek to realize our dreams and goals. Words are powerful, serving as both a blessing and a curse.

My vocal teacher, Diana Drew, in Canada helped me break through this obstacle, and shattering that false belief made a huge difference in my life. With her support, I discovered that I am a naturally good singer. Learning how to sing notes perfectly by using the right techniques, and most importantly believing in myself, changed my life. Today, my vocal coach and I share an amazing friendship of trust and mutual support. The result of now being able to sing is one of the precessional effects I experienced for myself for pursuing my goal of becoming an Instructor for the Money & You program. Another precessional effect I experienced was when my vocal teacher told me having me with her had also given her the opportunity to learn a lot from me and that I inspired her to continue to live her life to the fullest.

Learning how to accomplish the activities that satisfy my natural inclinations and deep desires has positively affected the way I make decisions. In other words, passion plus action equals a Purposeful Life. Passion and action fuel each other. My passion supports me in finding my purpose, and then fulfills it; my purpose nurtures my passion.

Recently, I met Oprah and had the opportunity to listen to her life story in person. I love what she said about Purpose – "Purpose is Spirit seeking Expression." I take that to mean it is just our Spirit seeking expression in this world and that is what I discovered about myself. Speaking and training are some of the ways my Spirit expresses itself. Perhaps ask yourself, where can you fully express yourself? Who are you when you do so? That is your purpose. Yes it is that simple and yet very profound.

Living A Life Of Essence: Human Doing Vs Human Being

Every day, I see so many people driving to work or some other place where they just have to be. Traffic is horrendous in Kuala Lumpur, in Toronto and in many other parts of the globe. I can't help but wonder – why do so many of us endure an hour or two or three of crawling slowly along in traffic just to get somewhere? Does this desire spring from our deep affinity with our work or have we just grown accustomed to the idea and the habit of going to the office to get through the day because we have to?

Many of us are just working for the sake of sustaining the life we're living, not the life we dreamed of or desire to live. We keep ourselves busy doing all sorts of things, but the busyness really derails our ambitions and goals. We think we're doing these things to gain happiness, but we're receiving anything but that. Instead, we flood our systems with cortisol. We feel increasing anxiety. We get grumpy a lot, even angry, and our productivity suffers. So do our personal relationships.

Being happy is never about what you have in life. Often, we think that having things will bring us happiness, but once we have them, we realize they are temporal.

When you are:
- Being human and accepting your limitations;
- Being comfortably with yourself and letting go of

judgments;
- Being with nature and breathing its beauty and balance;
- Being with your feelings whether they're positive or negative;
- Being able to connect fully with another human being;
- Being able to acknowledge and know that you are ENOUGH.

These are the moments in life in which one discovers true happiness. Remember that only when you are able to experience fully every moment of your life by being present in it do you truly live.

Our goals in life change as we grow and move forward through many different phases. Yet, may you always keep in mind that the *essence* of your existence will remain the same. You are born to love, to share joy. You will experience this one way in your twenties, another way in your forties and so on.

I also believe that Purpose is being in your essence. It's being who you are in this world. My purpose is PLAY, so I bring play to everything I do! In this process, I can see myself as being beauty, being joy, being creation itself, and I share that in everything I do, with everyone I meet, and everywhere I go.

You have the power to choose your purpose in life. Will you slow down, gaze within, and connect with the real essence of your existence? Just imagine that Being Joy is your purpose. How will you behave? How will you be with another person? How will you be in the office?

This is powerful. Can you become your purpose? How?

When you're being, you become your purpose. Your purpose is to experience life and expand into love.

So, my friends, let me say it again to each of you, yes! You can achieve your goals. In doing so, you can and will create great benefits for others, and you'll live exactly the life you've always wanted. Your purpose is your inner spirit seeking expression by you being who you are, your essence. Have a goal, a direction that gives you the clarity to move forward. This creates decisions that will keep you in motion and being on purpose.

Practices

Practice #1: *Where Can I Add The Greatest Value?*

Ask yourself: Where can you add the greatest value? How will you measure your life? People who don't stand for something, can easily fall for anything. Deciding how you want to measure your life means taking a stand for something and then living your life in alignment with it. Ultimately, living with purpose means focusing on things that matter most and are in alignment with your core values. What matters the most to you?

Practice #2: *Discover Your Core Values*

What are your deepest values? Write them down. By knowing your core values, you understand what matters most to you and how to best serve yourself and others on purpose.

Practice #3: *Your Message*

If you could get a message across to a large group of people: Who would those people be? What would your message be? This exercise could give you some insights into what drives you and serves you, which allows you to live on purpose.

Practice #4: *Causes You Believe in*

Given your talents, passions and values, how could you use these resources to serve, to help, to contribute? (To people, beings, causes, organization, environment, planet, etc.). What causes do you strongly believe in? Connect with?

Practice #5: *Check Your Passion Practices*

What you are passionate about gives you great insights into what your purpose is. Remember, passion plus action equals a Purposeful Life.

Practice #6: *Ask Others*

List 10 names of close friends and family and ask them what positive qualities they see in you. Write them down and pick the top 5 words that came up most frequently. Those are your essence. You can practice daily, taking one of the words and bring your essence and purpose to everything you are doing that day and see what is different in your life.

KEY #5: LIFE OF **POSSIBILITIES**

"I am where I am because I believe in all possibilities."
— Whoopi Goldberg

"You and I are essentially infinite choice-makers. In every moment of our existence, we are in the field of all possibilities where we have access to an infinity of choices."
— Deepak Chopra

Thoughts + Belief + Action = Results Of Possibilities

As all of you know, it is one thing to set our minds on a goal and an entirely different thing to act on and achieve it. It's great to let our imaginations run free and come up with a plan, but then comes the part that holds many of us back: taking action. A plan, after all, is just a plan; acting on that plan is living a life of purpose. Living a purposeful life is making a powerful, personal impact on others. It's doing things that support the healing of our sweet, wounded world.

If I had to sum up what creating possibilities in our lives is all about, I'd say it's willingness to connect one's thoughts with one's actions despite the unknown and it's outside of our comfort zone; it's just like putting together puzzle pieces spread all over the kitchen table to create a coherent whole. Thoughts plus Belief plus Action equal Results of Possibilities. For example, the Wright brothers believed in flight. They embraced and embodied their belief, took the necessary steps to make it happen, and succeeded beyond anyone's wildest dreams.

I'd like to share with you an experience I had that blessed me with a deeper understanding of the endless possibilities in our lives.

Recently, I traveled to Malaysia and Cambodia with my family and three children for several months. As a mother, I know how difficult it is to even visit the grocery store with small children, let alone travel to countries halfway around the globe for four months. Yet, my family and I were up for the challenge despite not knowing what to anticipate.

You see, I'm someone who accomplishes what she sets out to do especially since it sounded like a great adventure for my children and myself. I chose to focus on what possible positive outcomes that may come out of the trip rather than the possible negative outcomes. It wasn't easy to get everything together but it was well worth it. I even had to talk to the school principal to allow my kids to be away for four months. I was grateful that the principal and their teachers also saw the trip as a great opportunity for increasing my children's global awareness.

And after setting my mind to visiting Cambodia to give back to the community with my children, I took one step at a time and moved together with the universe's plan to make my vision a reality. I started reaching out to friends and family and asked for contacts of various foundations that are established in Cambodia. Within a short time, I was connected to Connie who then assisted us in planning the entire trip. She even planned a trip for herself to meet us there at SaoSary Foundation in Kampung Speu, Cambodia.

Sharing this vision with my children was an enriching experience for me. I informed them that we were taking a trip to a war-torn country. As we prepared, I also told them that we'd be staying at a shelter for a couple of days and that I'd love it if they spent time with the children, playing with them and sharing their knowledge.

I made it clear to my kids that I wanted them to see the world as it is. As a mother, I know that gaining first-hand experience in what's really happening in the world will greatly help all young people to appreciate and understand how fortunate they are in life. As we learn more about gratitude, it plants seeds of generosity in our hearts.

Realizing My Possibilities

By creating this life-changing event in my life and the lives of my children, I can only remember love and joy as a result. The entire experience just felt awesome.

Being able to visit Cambodia at last and getting the chance to support a foundation that truly walks its talk, changing the lives of many abused children is a really meaningful experience. I've been drawn to Cambodia for the longest time, and after that trip, I felt just as strongly about the country; I also discovered the joy that comes from being of service to others.

I know that the trip opened doors for my children, too. My children are beautiful in their own unique ways. Though my eldest son, Josiah, the adventurous one, was primed to go, my second-eldest, Jordan, was a little apprehensive about visiting new environments that were outside his comfort zone. As for my youngest child, Joy, well, she was just raring to go. In the end, I was more than pleased with the way they all adjusted and handled the trip.

On our first day, my boys were shy and somewhat uncomfortable, unlike Joy. I know that in addition to the unconventional environment, their difficulty communicating with the local children proved to be an additional challenge for them. But our second day came as a wonderful surprise for Zach and I. After leaving our kids at the shelter to interact more with the children, we found on returning that they were enjoying themselves to the point that they did not want to leave. I'm very happy that my children were able to overcome their shyness and make friends with the kids at the shelter.

The next day, Jordan had the wonderful idea of bringing fruits for their new friends. He had learned that fruit was a luxury for those kids. Yes, his parents were so proud of him! On the third day, we brought local cakes, which were thoroughly enjoyed by everyone. In fact, those cakes seemed to disappear within seconds of our arrival!

I am so proud of my children for what they were able to achieve during our short visit to Cambodia. It was a pleasure to see how, each in their own way, gracefully offered and accepted kindness and friendship. The entire experience was a clear affirmation of how truly blessed I am. The universe allowed me to make the journey and create meaningful experiences for my children and myself that all of us shall cherish for the rest of our lives. Also, I learned all over again that anything is possible as long as you believe and have faith in it. Projecting your thoughts and actions, then taking appropriate action, leads to living a visionary life.

We continued to travel around South East Asia for the next three months. We visited Singapore, Malaysia, Indonesia and Thailand. It was an unforgettable trip for the whole family.

Living A Life Without Limits

Possibilities are nothing more than what's out there waiting to be discovered in our lives. If we believe in the goodness of the universe, our hearts calmly sing that anything can be achieved. Opening a world of possibilities in every area of our lives begins with combining positive thoughts and a firm belief as we inch step-by-step closer to our dreams. As we know from the law of attraction, we hold the power to manifest our intentions and thoughts.

And yet, awakening the endless possibilities in our lives doesn't happen only through visualization. Setting our thoughts free through visualization will not be enough to guide us in reaching our dreams. Crafting our dreams into being begins with seeing, feeling and believing that we already possess what we desire. Believing is powerful.

To believe is to have faith and a clear vision. The walls we erect with negative thoughts hinder us from attracting the goodness we'd like to experience in our lives. These blocks are the negative stories of past trauma that stop us from being who we are. They are like the brake pedal in your car; when you step on the brake and the gas at the same time, you are going nowhere! It is important to seek what these blocks are and take on practices of clearing or removing them (At the appendix of this book, I have included various type of clearing methods/modalities that you can explore and experience).

I noticed that my life started transforming and a major factor was my openness to experience these various clearing modalities. In the process, learned a lot about myself and my subconscious beliefs that didn't serve me. Here are some examples; "I have to work hard for money", "Men are not trustworthy", "Friends leave me once we get too close", "I don't deserve a loving relationship", "I don't matter", and many more. For example, I realized why it was so difficult in my relationship. I didn't trust him from the beginning. It wasn't him. This one discovery started improving my relationship not only with my partner, but with others, too. I felt more secure and safer, definitely happier. Everything in my life started improving.

When we're happy, when inner joy is brimming over, the peace that springs from our strong beliefs sends waves of positivity and love that bring us closer to our heart's desire. It is only through growing our genuine belief in life, in others, and ourselves that we truly find the strength to take the first step. Let us not restrict ourselves by thinking that the law of attraction begins and ends with visualization. Never forget that we live in our own worlds, and we are the ones who hold the golden keys that unlock the diverse possibilities of our lives.

Make the conscious choice to send out positive thoughts as you draw strength from your firm belief. Then you will endure and enjoy every step of the way towards your dream. Never allow yourself to be blinded by the pains of the past or the uncertainty of the future. Know that we see the world through our own filters.

Curving Your Path

While creating endless possibilities in our lives, it helps to remember that nothing happens overnight. Even a seed must germinate at the beginning of its journey.

There are many factors that conjoin to transform vision into reality. The first factor is trust. Being able to trust that possibilities do exist creates a strong foundation for the life we intend to live. Trust must be cultivated from within before it can be shared with others. We must learn to trust our selves and others every step of the way. Thriving and growing in abundance springs from a deep sense of trust that something bigger than us supports us through our journey in this life. This process requires faith in trust.

Another important factor in creating possibilities is action. Without it, all that we have are unwritten wishes and dreams that can easily be blown away by the wind. When coupled with belief and trust, our actions become more meaningful and the cup of possibilities begins to fill in our lives. Finally, we need the courage to take the first step – courage to overcome our fears and take our first move towards creating and bringing possibility to our lives.

You may discover additional factors in your journey, but keep in mind that the power resides in our present moment, not in missed opportunities of the past, or in the future that we are so eagerly building. Every possibility begins with one action – that conscious and clear choice that we make today.

Empowering 'YOU'

Receiving is also an important concept in unlocking

possibilities in our lives. Knowing what we deserve and willingly opening our hearts to receive what the universe offers is very important.

More often than not, the gift of life has been sitting right there in front of us for the longest time. Yet, we fail to perceive these blessings. We begin to wonder mindlessly why we are living unfortunate lives. Not being able to see and accept the wonderful gifts of life always erects blockages in the thread of endless possibilities.

Once again, believing in our positive thoughts and what could be are powerful drivers of bringing our vision to life. Failure to believe sends mixed signals to the universe about our fears, and those fears simply create confusion.

Think of it as sending radio signals. If you intend to play the sound of music, and half-way through you begin to doubt whether you're playing the right song, then chances are you'll just give up and switch to a different tune.

Losing faith in your dreams and vision is a sure-fire way to fail to realize your limitless possibilities.

So, always keep in mind that you hold the key. You are the driver of your life, and the power to make your visions come true is within you.

The Choice Is Yours

Commitment - Make the decision to move forward in life. It's all about showing up every day and taking action. Being true to our word and continuing to be present in our lives, despite the challenges, is exactly what empowers us. This strengthens our commitment to life and the endless possibilities that we all deserve.

Responsibility - Take ownership of everything in your life. Blaming others is one of the easiest things to do amidst failure and despair, but in these times, it is best to take a good look at how we've created the results that we see. Avoiding the urge to justify and to give excuses supports us greatly in moving forward by allowing us to learn from our mistakes. Apologizing for our mistakes leads us to a better version of ourselves. I finally understood what Buckminster Fuller meant when he said, "Mistakes are only sins when not admitted". It is because we failed to see a mistake as mistake and learning experience and come to see it as fault or error and since we felt wrong or bad for making the mistake, we carry on the burden of it within us. And that is how it becomes a sin.

So, it is important to forgive yourself for the mistake and take it as a learning experience and let go. Then we can move forward. Yes, there are consequences to our mistakes. However, that is how as a human being, we learn. We learn through mistakes and course corrections.

Answer the call of life with only a yes or a no.

Declaration empowers each one of us to create endless possibilities. Declaration is consciously choosing an outrageous goal, out of our reality box to expand beyond our comfort zone. The power to create in our lives flows from this. There is a greater force at work that guides us in our pursuit of abundance. When you are on purpose, you create possibilities to experience that lead to your purpose.

Practice positive affirmation and visualization to unlock all things possible in your life. Request the support of people around you to provide support in this process.

It is by making a choice and a conscious effort to

believe, trust, receive, commit, and be responsible that we make all things possible in our lives. The power of endless possibilities in our lives comes from keeping the faith.

Practices

Practice #1: *DreamBoard*

Create a dream board that embraces and embodies your purpose. List what your dreams are. Remember to dream BIG! Start looking for photos or pictures that represent your dream and create your dream board. As much as this may not sound like it will work, it works.

I personally have created several dream boards and see many things on my dream boards became my reality especially one where I had Oprah Winfrey with me. I finally met her in person and took a great photo together in 2013. Make sure you put your dream board at a place that is visually accessible to you daily.

Practice #2: *Choose To Experience*

If you desire to own a luxury car, visit a dealership and test-drive the car you desire. Make your dream a full-body experience. This will support you in manifesting it into reality.

Practice #3: *Affirmation Exercise*

Sit quietly and ground yourself. When you're ready, open your journal and write down your affirmations ('I am beautiful', 'I love peach cobbler', 'I am a terrific listener',

'I am wealthy', for example). If you can, fill a page or more with life-affirming, inspiring affirmations. How does your list make you feel? Perhaps you'd enjoy printing some of them out and tacking them to your wall where you can see them every day. This will keep the positive energy flowing all around you.

A fun variation of this exercise is to do it with someone else, usually a loved one or close friend. But rather than compiling a list of affirmations about yourself, make a list about your exercise partner ('X is a great cook!', 'X is a terrific kisser', 'X really listens to me deeply', and so on). When you're finished writing, share your lists with each other. Don't be surprised if you enjoy the added benefit of rich communal laughter.

Practice #4: *Choices*

Practice being aware of choices that are available to you. Be mindful of how you choose. What are your choices based on? For example, do you choose something to please others or yourself? Pay attention to your thoughts and inner voices. This is a great insight discovery process.

Practice #5: *Creative Visualization Exercise*

Lie down on the floor, on your couch or bed, and close your eyes. Just lie there quietly in the silence for several minutes (five, ten, fifteen). If you could play some light music in the background would be great. Music activates our right brain and allows us to access our creative mind. Focus on your breath initially. Then, allow your mind to wander. Don't try to control your thoughts. Just be. You can use a timer if you'd like to set the end time of your reflection. When the time's up, write down in your journal the visualizations that came to you (at least those you can remember!).

Reflect on this list. Which of your visualizations surprise you? Do any trouble you? Why? Which speak to your long-term goals, your dreams and aspirations? And if you fall asleep during the lying-down part of this exercise, that's ok! It means you're tired and need a nap. That's ok, too! There is no right and wrong in the process of playful inquiry.

Practice #6: *Responsibility And Commitment Exercise*

What is your relationship to responsibility and commitment? When you think of responsibility what comes to your mind? Write it down. Same with commitment, what comes to your mind? Do you pay attention to this? How do you do it? Where in your life have you taken responsibility or not taken responsibility? Where in your life have you committed fully and not remained true to your commitment? Remember to forgive yourself for the past mistakes if they show up in this exercise. Choose to let go and choose to recommit or take on responsibility that works for you and others.

Practice #7: *Bless Things*

Bless your clothes, your food, the people who prepare it, those who made your furniture and car, the sidewalks you use, everything! Visualize all being filled with substance from the universe. Manifest the unmanifested! When we begin to bless others and things we are sending information to the Universe and saying we are abundant and we believe that there is enough abundance in the Universe for all things.

KEY # 6: CREATING **PRECIOUS** RELATIONSHIPS

"Walking with a friend in the dark is better than walking alone in the light." – Helen Keller

Loving Yourself And Loving Others With A Difference

Anything and everyone is precious, like a gemstone. They are important, beautiful and one of a kind. This uniqueness distinguishes each in the universe, and it makes them dear to my heart.

Of course, I am one of them! The more I've learned to love myself, the more I've learned to love everything else—all that make up this beautiful world we share. In my life, my children are precious, and so is every fellow human being on the planet. It is very easy to think that I'm looking at the world and my relationships through rose-tinted glasses, and that is the only reason that I am able to see things in a brighter light. But honestly, my relationships are far from perfect. I used to be a very angry person who brought up my eldest child by using conventional parenting methods that I had inherited from generations of tradition.

My pursuit of learning and the diverse experiences that unleashed my personal growth, taught me to become a better parent. I learn a lot from my children. They serve as a reminder to me to check in on my own ego. My children openly share with me about what is going on in their lives. This is through trust and respect we have built throughout the years. I've learned to apologize to my kids, to see that I am taking care of them while they are on this earth, and they don't 'belong' to me.

They are here as their very own beings and I am responsible to take care of them in the initial years and to assist them in discovering their true essence and let them soar and grow into their purpose here. My children and I have an amazing bond and they continue to fill my heart with joy and love.

On this journey of love, I have also grown closer to my parents. Though giving hugs is not a high priority for many Asian families, I have learned to give my parents hugs and connect with them on a deeper level. I strive to meet them now in a place of genuine love and respect, which I openly share with them. Gone are the days when I felt that it was my obligation to be a silent, 'good' and 'obedient' daughter. This has been a good transition for me, and it has been a wonderful transition for them, too.

Demonstrating your love for others draws their love for you out into the open, into the fresh air and sunshine. When love is flowing, unobstructed, back and forth, then possibilities become clearer and the whole world shimmers with positive energy.

The Dawn Of New Relationships

I was in my late teens when I realized how important relationships really are. Relationships weren't just accidental arrangements that came and went, or good or bad deals that nobody was responsible for, or that anybody could be blamed for when they went bad. Instead, I began to see relationships as a creation process of experiences, lessons and memories that will always be with me, no matter who I think I am at a given moment, or wherever I may go. That was a huge breakthrough for me, and from then on, I made a conscious decision to cherish my relationships with others.

It wasn't always easy. Of course, I made wrong turns and said hurtful things to other people. But at the end of the day, I learned how to recognize those shortcomings and make course corrections faster and faster. It all contributed to my deepening as a human being. It enriched my personal growth. I discovered that every mistake is an opportunity to be better. I have learned to acknowledge my shortcomings when they arise in my relationships. Now I always aim to treat people with the utmost love and respect, just the way I want them to treat me.

There are no good or bad relationships in this life. It is best to think of every relationship as a journey you enjoyed or didn't enjoy. This healthy perspective on how we interact with others supports our growth in all areas, including meaningful relationships with family, friends and others. Keep in mind that relationships reflect the goodness and pain that reside deep within our hearts and bodies as we learn more about ourselves and learn from the mistakes we make. It serves as an opportunity for us to learn about the triggers and blocks within us.

On Self-Love And Being Selfish

I used to think that putting myself first was wrong. It just seemed selfish to care for myself first, putting my needs above the needs of others. But in feeling that way, I was making a common mistake. You may have made this mistake many times, too! The mistake I made was this: confusing self-love with being selfish.

Doing anything to satisfy our own interest without regard for others is definitely being selfish. Yet, self-love is on an entirely different plane because it acknowledges the reality that we have to care for ourselves in order to love others more effectively. This life lesson is certainly the most important one I've learned on my journey of personal growth.

I know that many of us have been raised to believe that loving ourselves over our brothers and sisters is not right. We've been trained to believe it lacks integrity and brings up our worst grasping qualities. This line of thought inevitably locks us into a cycle of grudging obligation towards others. Even as we strive to do beneficial work for others, we acknowledge, if we're honest, building resentment and anger, which sometimes escalates to rage.

If we want to avoid this cycle, we need to remember that our first obligation is to ourselves. We can't serve others well if we don't serve ourselves first. Think of the oxygen mask in the airplane. You are always told to put yours on first before assisting another. This is good advice for survival! Love yourself first so that you will be able to love others.

Also consider that we bully ourselves worse than we bully anyone else. We're hard on ourselves! Often, we don't allow room for any mistakes. I know that I've gone through periods in my life where I'm constantly pushing myself, not taking breaks when I 'should', and not taking restorative time when I needed it. I was last on my list, and I was incredibly mean to myself! I was my own worst bully. Yet, I have been able to turn that around. I know that once we love ourselves, we're able to be present, have fun, live in joy and possibility. Today, I'm a strong advocate for all to be madly in love with themselves. We are most precious to ourselves!

So, take care of yourself first, and please consider this. If you are tired, rest. Compromising yourself for others will encourage feelings of resentment that hinder the growth of relationships. These relationships have terrific potential. They can become precious in your life, but that won't happen if you stumble in to them with the wrong intentions, or for the wrong reasons.

Taking care of yourself will go a long way towards making sure that those relationships are properly cultivated. Remember that taking care of yourself first will always be as important as taking care of others. And please, do it in that order.

Relationships That Matter

We all want our relationships to matter. We want to be enriched by them, and we want to empower others by our presence in their lives. So, where does this mutual power come from? It comes from the ability to acknowledge what is precious in your own sweet life. It comes from being present and offering undivided trust as you become one with yourself, with others and most importantly, the universe.

Knowing which relationships and experiences are precious creates great support in our daily lives. It allows us to cherish each moment we live. It follows that we'll treat others, as well as ourselves, with love and respect that encourages genuine mutual understanding through compassion.

Through my amazing relationships, I noticed how much more they have added to my life, opportunities to experience love, joy, excitement, enthusiasm, fun, laughter, sadness, grief, hurt, pain, frustration, anger, disappointment, deep soulful connection, appreciation, passion and compassion and the experiences and adventures of life. To me, I regard our experience on earth like visiting a theme park, we can choose to just enter the theme park and not take any rides and just wait till it's closing time or we can choose to experience different rides which we may or may not like; however, at least we can go home and say we had experiences.

Precious relationships make us better individuals. I am grateful for all of my relationships. I know I've learned so much from each of them, and I've learned to be grateful, which is the celebration that comes of living with a truly open and loving heart and spirit. Gratitude creates in us the desire for balanced reflection.

For instance, what meaningful connections have you created that are important to you?

Practices

Practice #1: *Reflect On Personal Relationships*

Sit quietly for a few minutes and reflect on your

personal relationships. In your journal, make a list of those relationships you feel really good about. Then jot down a list of those relationships that make you sad. You can list relationships in the past as well as the present.

Think about the relationships that make you feel good. What do you love about them? Why did they do well? What could you have done to manage those relationships better?

Think about the relationships that make you feel sad. What about them that disappointed you? Why did they fail or suffer? What could you have done to manage those relationships better, perhaps leading to a more positive outcome?

Next, how do you think the other person in those sad relationships would feel? Imagine being them. What would they say if they were writing in your journal?

Practice #2: *Gratitude*

Every morning when you wake up, and every evening before you sleep, write a list of those things, events and people you're grateful for including yourself. A friend, Jenny Craig, recently gave me a Grateful Ring to remind me of what I am grateful for in the moment and especially in moments that I feel challenged.

Practice #3: *Putting Self First*

Consider how you say no or yes to everything around you. Do you put others first? Consider how often you acknowledge yourself. Do you pay yourself first? In other words, whatever income you are making, do you put aside money for yourself; and do you trust yourself? Write down what comes to your mind when you reflect on these questions.

Practice #4: *Support And Acceptance*

How do you ask for support? Are you shy about it? Does it make you uncomfortable? How often do you ask for support? Do you expand your network of support?

It is always good to remember that no person is an island. None of us can lead a fulfilling life without the help of others. As human beings, we desire and even crave for community. Whether it's family members, friends, co-workers or strangers, we all need someone of whom we can ask for support, someone who can help us become centered and present in the current moment.

Are you accepting of what is, what comes your way, including the help of others? Acceptance is acknowledging things as they are instead of wanting to control or change the outcome. What are some things that are easier for you to accept and harder for you to accept? If there is anyone, who do you find difficult to accept? How come? What about this person that makes it difficult? Do know that this individual is giving you an opportunity to learn more about your inner pains and let them go.

Practice #5: *Trust And Letting Go*

Do you have trust issues? Take a deep look at what they are and why you hang on to them. How can you see yourself shedding that obstacle and begin developing trust?

How adept are you at letting go of things that no longer serve you?

Practice #6: *What Is Selfishness To You*

What does that word mean to you? In your journal, write down some examples of selfishness. Write about some specific instances when people were selfish around you. Then write down specific instances when you were selfish. Are there any areas in your life now where you feel you're acting selfishly? Or are you simply, and wisely, taking care of yourself?

What is the difference, to you, between selfishness and selflessness?

Everyone is capable of being selfish, and everyone is just as capable of being selfless. It's human nature to be both. Yet, we possess free will and choice, and we would all usually choose to be selfless rather than selfish. The point I want to make to you, though, is that selflessness does not mean sacrificing yourself. Not at all! You can and will be most effectively selfless after you've first taken care of your own emotional needs. Then you will assist others from a place of genuine compassion and caring. Your empathy will not be clouded by doubt and fear. Take care of yourself! Then reach out your helping and understanding hands to someone else.

That's when you'll truly love yourself, and then love others with a life-changing difference.

KEY #7: **PAY IT FORWARD** - GENEROSITY

"A life lived for others is the only life worth living."
– Albert Einstein

"We make a living by what we get, we make a life by what we give." – Sir Winston Churchill

Be Generous, Give Of Yourself

I have been active in charitable work for many, many years. This passion of mine began in my youth. I was inspired by Mother Teresa's decades of selfless work to open my own heart to those who are less fortunate than I.

Being blessed with the chance to experience wealth in my life is something that I am very thankful for. I am given the opportunity to have the capacity to buy what I desire and want, in addition to providing for my family. I also get the chance to shop for high-end labels (I get them more for their quality and durability) and travel from time to time. These aren't the be-all and end-all of my life, but they add variety and color to my existence, and that's a lovely thing!

Being in a position where I have the ability to give others and myself wonderful gifts has always given me a sense of joy. At one point, I realized that it didn't make me a better individual just to be able to travel and buy things. I also discovered that it was not enough to sustain and create the kind of happiness that is truly fulfilling. This feeling is not entirely new. I know of many friends and family members who have also gone through this experience, but I never fully understood its depth until I went through it myself.

Paying it forward is giving or sharing with another what you've received and having that individual do the same for the benefit of others. I learned that only when we are certain of our selves and who we are, can we begin to cease looking for love and happiness in external sources. All the designer clothes and vacations to exotic locales in the world will never buy you true happiness and peace of mind. Only contributing to humanity has the power to create a deep sense of lasting satisfaction in our lives.

On Giving And Gratitude

There are a couple of things that we have to learn in order to align these concepts in our daily lives. First of all, give back to ourselves with the sense of fulfillment we are able to create.

I believe that giving and receiving are necessary if we are to experience true happiness and fulfillment. Being open to others and learning how to receive works hand in hand with the ability to give because it allows the exchange to flow both ways.

Gratitude is another important concept to embrace if we

want to make a contribution to humanity. It is easy to gripe and whine about everything that we don't have in life. This can cause us to lose our focus. We become bitter and resentful, and we forget who we really are. Please keep in mind that when we are grateful for who we are and what we have, we take control of our lives and put the power in our own hands.

Compassion is essential, too. Compassion is being able to care for others with kindness and understanding. Empathy plays a significant role in demonstrating compassion by allowing us to extend ourselves. In this state of grace, we know what it's like to walk in another's shoes. We can literally feel their pain and suffering, and we want to do all that we can to alleviate them. Being able to share these feelings with others brings abundance and gratitude into our own lives.

Gratitude and compassion support every one of us as we strive to open our hearts and allow in a genuine experience of love in our lives.

The Experience And Expression Of Love

Personally, I believe that love really does make the world go round. I love my children. If I am in a relationship, I love my partner. I love my parents and siblings, and I love my close friends. I have also committed my life to loving others as I would be loved. Yet there is an opposite feeling that gets in the way of love and loving, and that is fear. Fear can eat away at our resolve and our best intentions. Just like you, I have felt and met my fears many times. Fear can stop love in its tracks. It can isolate us. It can even damage important relationships. Left to run amuck, fear can and will do great harm.

In truth, though, fear is also an opportunity. When fear arises, its presence gives us the opportunity to see it for what it really is—illusion. Fear is what we give in to when we subconsciously want to stop our progress. Fear is simply saying, 'I don't know what's around the bend, so I'll stop right here'. Fear encourages giving in and giving up.

We can give in to our fears, or we can face them and turn them into gold. How do we do that? One way is to consciously feel the fear and acknowledge it. It is when we push the fear away that it persists. When we acknowledge it, it dissipates. What is important is to take it another step forward, which is to move beyond the fear, and we do it by consciously creating other emotions like joy and gratitude. We have faith that possibilities are just around the corner. Love and fear can actually work together to expand our experience. We can experience fear to understand love as we go through our journey in life.

As human beings, we can express love in many ways. We get this emotion across to others through spoken words, texts, emails, Skype sessions, in-person actions, letters and even through our spiritual essence. We can make love connections in so many ways.

Of course, the love that we feel doesn't always have to be shared with another individual. Sometimes, it is more important for us to hone in on the experience of self-love. Remember? We can't truly love someone else before we truly love our selves. Many of us tend to forget that we, too, are individuals who need to be loved. It is when we love ourselves that we can learn to expand our hearts and let others in unconditionally.

Loving without conditions is the purest form of

unconditional love. This means loving, accepting love and offering love, without expectations of any kind. There are no requirements to deserve this kind of love because it accepts the other in his or her entirety without even a single expectation of being perfect or blameless. We are all perfect, we are all blameless, and we are all responsible. We are complete and whole; we are perfect as we are. We make choices, and then live by them. Choose wisely. Choose love.

By doing so, we tap into our capacity for experiencing and sharing our generosity. I think often of Mother Teresa. Every day in her life she met challenges by generously paying forward her personal generosity.

Our Currency Is Love

Paying it forward is a form of self-actualization that is achieved through the genuine sharing of love of oneself and others. When we completely realize our connection to other human beings, when we get it that we're all connected in the universe, and to the vast universe beyond our little place here on earth, then we are ready to contribute to humanity by giving, by feeling, by loving.

Just imagine your body. It is made up of trillions of cells, which are the 'mini', you. Each cell has its own unique function and capabilities and yet they are all part of you. That's what we are, we are all One. So when you see another human being, you are seeing an extension of you. Be kind, be considerate, be generous, be loving and be compassionate. We are meant to take care of each other with the power of love that we were born with.

Paying it forward is an act of love that flows from one

person to another. This flow is the river of humanity.

I would like to add that I personally believe minerals, plants and animals are living beings and they are part of us, too. So, please act lovingly to these fellow beings too.

Practices

Practice #1: *List Of Charitable Acts*

In your journal, make a list of the charitable acts you've done in the last week. Make another list for the last month, then for the last year.

What does your list look like? Does reviewing it bring up happy thoughts and memories? Are you troubled by anything? Were your motives clear as you contemplated, then followed through with these activities?

Perhaps you're dissatisfied with your list. Do you feel that you did not do enough? Were you appropriately taking care of yourself while you performed your good deeds? What might you do differently?

Practice #2: *Homeless People Or Street Beggars*

This exercise may make you uncomfortable, but it's a good one for you to try. Write in your journal a paragraph or two in which you lay out how you feel about encountering street beggars or homeless people. Most of us are so conflicted at those moments, so you needn't feel bad or alone if you notice that your response is a negative one. That's ok. Honesty is always the first best step to transformation and greater understanding. Write what you honestly feel and do. Do you always give money or food to a beggar? Do you rely on your intuition (*Is this person really in need, or not?*), or on your reaction to the way the beggar looks? Is it your policy never to give anything to beggars? Do you meet their eyes, or do you look away?

How does this process of writing about your reactions to street beggars strengthen or change your views?

Personally, I made a decision to give something to each beggar I meet. I've learned that no one wants to be on the street. People wind up there because of circumstances, some of which are beyond their control. I'm well aware of opinions that say beggars only use money to buy alcohol and drugs; some do. Those that do only know how to ease their pain in this addictive way. I don't condone their behavior; I'm compassionate about their living conditions.

Practice #3: *Become Love-Active*

This exercise requires you to leave your journal and favorite chair and go outside. After doing a little research, volunteer at a soup kitchen or youth hostel. Visit patients at a local hospital. Go in and see the residents at a retirement facility. Or walk a stretch of a rural highway and bag litter along the road.

Practice #4: *Commit Acts Of Kindness*

Do a simple act of kindness for someone you don't know. What will that be? Perhaps it is as simple as smiling at someone every day. Buy someone a coffee. Give someone a hug.

There are all kinds of things you can do to be more proactive in paying it forward. By doing so, you become love-active, and that love will return to you multifold!

HARNESSING YOUR **POWER**

"Freedom is not given to us by anyone; we have to cultivate it ourselves. It is a daily practice...no one can prevent you from being aware of each step you take or each breath in and breath out." – Thich Nhat Hanh

"I'm a strong believer that you practice like you play; little things make big things happen." – Tony Dorsett

What Do I Do Now?

At this point you might be asking, what's next? What doors in my life can I unlock with these powerful practices of living?

If you have these questions in mind then you are definitely heading in the right direction! In this bonus chapter, I'll guide you through getting a head start in harnessing your power to bring prosperity to your unique and special life. It's all about paying attention, being balanced. Trust and the proper focus take us far!

Before moving forward, let's resolve to keep in mind that lack of trust and the desire to be in control will inevitably complicate our lives with needless and negative obstacles. Wanting to take control is a fruit of fear. This can happen to any one of us when our present situation is under guard as a hostage of our past. Fighting fate to produce the results we desire never comes with a guarantee that it will erase our past failures and experiences. Those experiences, even the failures, are fertile ground we must till in order to achieve the bountiful harvest. We need to learn from our experiences and failures and let them go through a transformative process of trust and personal growth.

To trust is to listen to our inner voice. Our intuition is yearning to become our internal guidance system. All it takes to be positively activated is trust. Can you do that? Of course you can! Remember that all of us are only given a certain amount of time in this world to love and make a difference in our lives and the lives of others. Keeping this in mind supports and inspires us in striving to live a life of experience and service in the here and now.

Our experiences create memories. Each of us has the power consciously to choose the experiences that we savor and enjoy. We must sift through the sediment of our peak, low and in-between experiences, choosing to cherish what is good and sustaining, and disposing *of* that which does not serve and holds us back. When we succeed at that sifting process, we arrive at the point where we act from a place of empowerment. Standing confidently on that fertile ground, we are able to value and love ourselves as we ought to love. We are also capable of loving others.

Of course, each one of our experiences enriches us in different ways. The prosperity of our lives is crafted by our experiences in whichever way we classify them. At the end of the day, both the good and bad circumstances in our lives add up to the experiences that make us better individuals. Putting labels on those experiences only takes us away from the true happiness that we endeavor to discover.

There are endless roadblocks along this path, and our task is to navigate through all of them until we arrive at a clear field of progress in the moment. The journey is endless, and we recognize that it is endlessly fun, exciting and inspiring. What will you become today? What will you do?

Practice Can't Make You Perfect, But It Advances Your Goals

Consider an example. When you are playing tennis, you have to practice and train hard to become a master of the game. There are endless hours of hitting ground strokes against a backboard, and more hours on the court honing your serve and footwork. You must increase your stamina, sharpen your eyes and develop what I refer to as court sense—anticipating, feeling the game, letting it enter you unobstructed, and then trusting your body to do the rest.

The same rigorous training and practice apply to honing new knowledge and skills in any endeavor, be it work, play, family or relationships. You are ready to open doors to your path of discovery and personal growth.

This is important! Throughout your practice of these keys, allow yourself to make mistakes, and be aware that any mistakes you make along the way are just learning experiences. Welcome them. Sit with them. Be grateful for the opportunity they present you to become a better, more powerful and generous person.

Remember, too, to be gentle with yourself. Carefully direct and guide yourself as you make your way along your path of discovery. I know that many of us, including me, can be too hard on ourselves. I have beaten myself up many times, and never has it served me well. Seeking perfection is a noble pursuit. Yet, always keep in mind that the only thing in this life that's perfect is imperfection. What do I mean by this? It's simple and true. All of us are perfectly imperfect in our own ways, and that's what makes us unique.

Life can almost feel like an effortless journey if only we allow it to be so, if only we can learn to stay out of our way. None of us needs to struggle if we learn to trust the universe and ourselves, as well as everything and everyone we connect with. If we envision life as free-flowing water that seeks its own forms as it makes its way, it can remind us that everything will be okay. Though the water's path, like our lives, may turn and pool and wind around various obstacles, it, and we, will always continue on towards a potent destination.

Set up a group to share your practices. Write down what you've done and share them with others who have done likewise. Share a chapter every week, or every month.

Practicing the seven keys of powerful living has taught me to accept many diverse things in my life. It hasn't always been easy for me, but I have learned to accept what is with all my heart. I have done so without demanding it to be different than what it already is. I know that the universe is filled with abundance. I am grateful for the opportunity each new day and night offers me. I accept that all of us are on parallel journeys made up of many people, events and situations that we must navigate with trust, integrity and good faith. All we have to do is train ourselves to see the universe, and our lives, for what they are—a glorious field of ever-changing, positive possibilities.

YOU are the Power

In so many precious ways, I believe that these values work hand in hand with one another. Consciously practicing each one of these values allows us to kick-start the lives we want to lead. Everything we dream, and all that we desire for, is within reach. The life force wants nothing more than that we achieve it, that we reach and realize our goals. Always remember that the real power is within you and you alone. No one and nothing can hold you back! The life we desire is within all of us—full of vigor, energy and possibilities.

Lead yourself to prosperity. I'm not just talking about wealth, but prosperity in all areas of life—emotional, mental, spiritual, physical, financial and social. The prosperous road is within you, and it awaits your first brave step.

Go forth. Be adventurous. Be prosperous and social. Become the person you are!

OUR **PARTNERSHIP**

In this chapter, I invite you to partner with me. I intentionally left this portion blank because as we end this book, to me it's the new beginning of another book, which will be written by you. The next author. It is your turn to create your story and your legacy and share it with the world. I am so honored to have you finish up my book and be in partnership with me. I know that you can create your life exactly the way you want it to be because I have experienced it and as I have said earlier, if I can, so can you. I am just an ordinary girl living an extraordinary life because I choose to do so.

So take a moment, breathe, get present and if you like, play. Evoke your positive emotions, and begin to write down what you see happening in your life 5 years from now. Write it down in present tense and just add 5 more years to it. Write down what you see around you, who is around, and where are you are living. What are you doing? What is your career? What impact are you creating in the world? What are people saying to you? What are they seeking you for? Who are you being? Describe your success (Personally, to me success means having a life with inner peace, love, joy and freedom and having many wonderful connections and relationships with others and with the Universe). How are you feeling most of the time?

Write down what had happened in the last 5 years leading to this very date. How has your life changed? What changed? What was there more of in your life? Less of? What have you let go? What forgiveness work have you done? How did you find and understand your purpose and discover your passion? What are your passion and purpose? What possibilities showed up in your life because you made a decision and a choice to see the world differently, especially after reading this book? How often did you play? Describe how you nurture your inner child and love your inner child and accept your inner child? Describe how you have forgiven those you've wronged and those who have wronged you. Describe how you practice being present every day. Write down which community or communities you are sharing your talents, skills and wisdom with. Which charities are you supporting? Did you get married? Did you get divorced? Describe your romantic relationships. Share how you are feeling most of the time – peace, calm, loving, joy, safe, etc.

As you complete this chapter, know that it is Possible! As long as you set your intention clear, send it to the Universe, believe it and begin to do the inner work and practice some of the keys I have shared with you in this book. Remember to post this last chapter somewhere visible to you and visualize, feel and know it is real. I send you my love and I wish you all the best in everything. You are a magnificent being coming to planet Earth to experience a magical journey. It takes you to create a meaningful life of love and power.

AFTERWORD:
BE A **LOVE WARRIOR**
LEAD A **POWERFUL LIFE**

Join me as a Love Warrior. Be part of the movement. Share this book with your friends and family, create conversations with people about the keys you learned in this book and inspire others by leading a powerful life by demonstrating your powerful love. Ultimately, we are all loving beings, we have just forgotten who we are. I truly believe when we come together and live with love and purpose, we are able to impact others to do the same for themselves. With this, we are able to create peace in the world.

To continue to receive updates on new practices, please go to my website and sign up for my newsletter.

Finally, please share your stories and journey with me. I look forward to hearing from you.

Love and peace to you ☺

ABOUT THE AUTHOR

Annie Lim, PhD, is a fun and loving person. She has had good days and bad days. Some days she thinks she is the best mom on earth; on other days, the worst mom ever.

Her husband thinks she is a great cook, yet she is unsure about that.

She laughs, cries, gives and receives hugs and kisses and loves to play. At times, she gets scared, yet most of the time, she is courageous. She enjoys challenges in her businesses and also enjoys an awesome day at the spa with her friends. She is often asked how she keeps herself slim. Well, having to run after three amazing children definitely helps!

Annie Lim used to be quiet and shy, but now she speaks up and speaks her truth. She enjoys her life, being at peace and joyful most of the time. She is a philanthropist, social entrepreneur and a Love Warrior at heart.

At her core, she is just a human being with different life experiences.

To learn more about Annie, visit her website:

DrAnnieLim.com

 / DrAnnieLim    @DrAnnieLim

Made in the USA
Columbia, SC
15 April 2019